SHIPPING MADE ~~SIMPLE~~ PROFITABLE

Why Understanding Logistics (10 steps) is the Key to Bigger Profits in Exports & Imports

SHIPPING MADE ~~SIMPLE~~ PROFITABLE

Why Understanding Logistics (10 steps) is the Key to Bigger Profits in Exports & Imports

Deepak Bhadwarya

Available on amazonkindle

Worldwide Published by

Pendown Press
PREMIUM BUSINESS PUBLISHER

PENDOWN PRESS LLP

An ISO 9001 & ISO 14001 Certified Co.,

Regd. Office: 3767A, Kanhaiya Nagar,

Tri Nagar, Delhi-110035

Ph.: 8130886000, 9650072927, 8595249536

E-mail: info@pendownpress.com

Branch Office: 1A/2A, 20, Hari Sadan, Ansari Road,

Daryaganj, New Delhi-110002

Ph.: 011-45794768

Website: PendownPress.com

Edition: 2025

Price: ₹ 299

ISBN: 978-93-6338-585-6

Layout and Cover Designed by Pendown Graphics Team

Printed and Bound in India by Thomson Press India Ltd.

DEDICATION

To Indian exporters and importers who wish to contribute to the Indian economy by producing and promoting the Indian brand name internationally.

Table of Contents

Preface

I'm not a writer by profession—I'm just someone who's spent 25 years working closely with Indian exporters and importers. Over the years, I've seen people struggle with delays, mistakes, and unnecessary stress—all because logistics was misunderstood, or not given the attention it deserves.

This book isn't written with heavy words or complex theories. It's written straight from the heart.

I've always believed that if I've learned something the hard way, and if that learning can save someone else from facing the same trouble, then it's my duty to share it.

That's exactly what this book is meant to be—a helpful companion. Not a textbook. Not a lecture. Just a guiding hand for business owners, staff, or anyone who wants to understand how to avoid losses and run smoother import-export operations.

Many people get scared just hearing the word "logistics." But it's not a monster. With the right understanding, it becomes your strongest business partner.

This book is especially for small and medium business owners—those who manage most things on their own, without fancy teams or big budgets. If this book can make your journey even a little easier, then every hour I spent writing it is worth it.

Thank you for giving your time to this book.

I truly hope it serves you well.

Warm regards,

Deepak Bhadwarya

Preface

Author's Corner

Having spent **25 years** in the logistics industry, I've worked closely with exporters & importers across India—from the ports of Mumbai to the industrial belts of Chennai and the air cargo hubs of Delhi. I've witnessed firsthand the challenges Indian exporters and importers face.

When I first entered the logistics fraternity, I found it incredibly exciting—it felt like the lifeblood of the economy. Logistics plays a vital role by ensuring the availability of essential raw materials from other countries & helping India deliver world-class products to the world.

Back then, logistics was in a very basic form. Most operations were manual, with little transparency or process visibility. While working with a Custom House Agent (CHA), I observed that there was heavy dependency on individuals preparing export and import documents manually. A single mistake at this stage could lead to major delays at customs. Similarly, issues with shipping lines often resulted in costly penalties in the form of detention and demurrage.

I've worked across the spectrum—CHA firms, shipping lines, and even in IATA (airlines)—and one thing remained constant: **the gap between customer expectations and what was being delivered. This gap has always inspired me to do more and be more useful to customers.**

Though I already held an MBA, I pursued a Post Graduate Diploma in Retail Supply Chain Management from IIM Indore. This helped me gain deeper insight into the challenges my customers faced and allowed me to design better service offerings to meet their needs.

But life took an unexpected turn. After the sudden closure of Transpole Logistics Pvt. Ltd., I had two choices: search for a new job or start my own venture. At that time, the job market was slow, and opportunities were limited. So, I took a leap of faith and started my own company—despite having no prior business experience.

The initial years were financially and operationally tough. But with a "Customer First" approach and a deep desire to serve, we managed to stand strong. I've always felt a sense of gratitude toward this industry, and that's what inspired me to write this book.

I know I cannot personally reach every business owner, so this book is my way of giving back—a simple guide covering **10 key procedures** that can help you avoid financial losses and procedural delays.

This book is especially written for small and medium-sized business owners who do not have a dedicated logistics department and often manage things on their own—or rely on accounts staff who may not have full knowledge in this field.

Acknowledgements

First and foremost, I would like to thank my parents for their unconditional love and the nurturing environment they provided during my early childhood. Their support laid the foundation for me to grow into an independent and confident individual.

I am deeply grateful to **Akshar Yadav Sir**, who helped me believe that we are here to serve society. This book is one such humble attempt in that direction.

To my wife, **Mrs. Neeru Singh,** you've been my steady hand through every storm and success. Your ability to balance home and support me with such wisdom and grace is something I deeply admire. Thank you for being my strongest support system.

I am also grateful to **Mr. Viral Zaveri** and **Mr. Vikas Kaila**, whose constant motivation has always inspired me to give my best.

A special thanks to all my staff and the entire **Fluid Global Logistics LLP** team for their feedback, suggestions, and encouragement throughout this journey. Your support gave me the confidence to publish this book with the hope that it proves helpful to many.

I am sincerely thankful to my customers for their continued trust and support. I also extend my gratitude to **Mr. Amit Banthia** for his valuable support and faith in me.

Lastly, I would like to thank **Mr. Dinesh Verma** and the entire **Pendown Press** team for their support and insightful suggestions throughout the creative process.

Introduction: Why Optimizing Your Logistics Strategy Matters

In today's global marketplace, logistics isn't just a support function—it's the backbone of international trade. For Indian exporters and importers, it plays a far greater role than simply transporting goods from Point A to Point B. It influences everything—from cost efficiency and customer satisfaction to brand reputation and long-term sustainability.

Every successful trade transaction depends on a smooth flow of operations—clear documentation, timely movement, coordinated efforts between suppliers, freight forwarders, customs, and buyers. One misstep, one delay, or one error in paperwork can set off a chain of losses. Yet, many businesses—especially small and mid-sized ones—tend to overlook the power of an optimized logistics strategy.

In real terms, this means more than just negotiating lower freight rates. It means knowing when to consolidate shipments, choosing the right shipment mode, staying up-to-date with policy changes, and having reliable partners to avoid costly surprises. It also means planning ahead, avoiding last-minute rushes, and building systems that prevent chaos.

This book is not about theories. It's about practical, field-tested insights gained from years of working with Indian businesses across ports, airports, ICDs, and customs offices. It's written to help you understand the importance of logistics in simple language—and to equip you with the clarity to avoid common pitfalls that quietly eat into your margins.

Because in trade, every rupee saved in logistics is a rupee earned in growth.

Why this Book?

As a logistics expert, my relationship with my customers goes far beyond just transactions. They deserve the very best in logistics services. If I fail to meet their expectations, I feel that the true purpose of my work—and my life—remains incomplete.

This book is my way of giving back to the logistics fraternity. Since I can't reach every business owner personally, I've created this practical guide with **10 essential procedures** to help avoid common financial and operational delays.

It's especially written for **small and medium-sized business owners** who often manage logistics themselves or depend on accounts staff with limited knowledge in this area.

These lessons, drawn from years of hands-on experience, are designed to help exporters streamline operations, reduce costs, and grow confidently in today's global market.

So, let's not wait any longer and begin our journey toward smarter logistics.

Why This Book?

CHAPTER 1

Hidden Logistics Costs That Are Eating Into Your Trade Profits

Logistics inefficiencies are silent profit killers for our **fraternity**. In the effort to reduce logistics costs, we often chase low freight rates—without realizing the **hidden charges, delays, and supply chain bottlenecks** that directly and indirectly drain our energy and margins.

Common Logistics Mistakes

- Unnecessary handling fees
- High inland transport costs
- Customs clearance delays due to faulty documentations

Case Study: ₹ 15 Lakhs Per Annum Saved Through Smart Logistics

One of our customers, Metronex Steel Corporation (*real name has been withheld at the customer's request*), a top producer of reinforcement bars, was facing major logistics hurdles due to **decentralized procurement.** This led to fragmented shipments, high transportation costs, and delayed deliveries.

Challenges Faced

- No centralized control over procurement and logistics
- Higher transportation and container costs
- Extended lead times
- Increased risk of **detention and demurrage charges** at destination ports
- Overall financial losses

Solution Provided

- Collaborated with domestic vendors
- Developed a region-wise consolidation plan
- Grouped shipments from nearby vendors
- Reduced the number of containers through strategic consolidation

Implementation Process

- Close coordination among Metronex Steel Corporation, its vendors, and Fluid Global Logistics
- Clear packaging and labeling guidelines were established
- Robust tracking systems were implemented for timely monitoring

Results & Outcomes

- Achieved **30% reduction in logistics costs**
- Cost savings through region-wise shipment consolidation
- Reduced lead time from supplier locations to destination
- Effectively mitigated risks of detention and demurrage

6 Smart Ways to Cut Hidden Logistics Costs

1. **Audit & Optimize Costs**: Avoid overpaying for freight, warehousing, and customs.
2. **Consolidate Shipments**: Reduce customs fees and transportation costs by bundling goods.
3. **Choose the Right Freight Mode**
    - **Sea Freight**: Best for cost-effective bulk shipments
    - **Air Freight**: Ideal for urgent, high-value goods
    - **Hybrid Approach**: Balance speed and cost
4. **Optimize Routing & Carrier Selection**: Smarter routes mean faster delivery and better cost control.
5. **Master Customs Regulations**: Prevent penalties and delays with accurate documentation and compliance.
6. **Partner with a Freight Expert**: Improve decision-making, reduce risks, and enhance supply chain performance.

Logistics: A Competitive Advantage, Not Just a Cost

- Boost profits
- Ensure on-time deliveries
- Stay competitive in global trade

Don't let hidden costs eat your margins—optimize your logistics today!

CHAPTER 2

Maximizing Trade Incentives: Are You Losing Money on Imports & Exports?

The Importance of Trade Incentives

Government schemes provide financial relief to importers and exporters by reducing duties, offering tax exemptions, and improving cash flow. Yet many businesses fail to claim these benefits—often due to lack of awareness, over-reliance on CHAs (Customs House Agents), or documentation errors.

These missed opportunities can silently eat into your profits.

Key Import & Export Incentives

➢ **Duty Drawback & Remission Schemes**

- **For Exporters:** Receive refunds on customs duties paid for imported inputs used in manufacturing goods for export.
- **For Importers:** Benefit from duty-free imports of raw materials and capital goods under Advance Authorization & EPCG (Export Promotion Capital Goods) schemes.

- **Common Issues:** Missing compliance deadlines or using incorrect HS code classification can lead to penalties or lost refunds.

➢ **IGST Refunds & Exemptions**

- **For Exporters:** Can ship goods under LUT (Letter of Undertaking) without paying IGST upfront.
- **For Importers:** Exemptions available under EPCG, SEZ, and Advance Authorization schemes.
- **Common Issues:** Delays in refund claims can cause serious cash flow disruptions.

➢ **Special Tariff Concessions under FTAs & PTAs**

- **For Importers:** Reduced or zero customs duties available through Free Trade Agreements (FTAs) and Preferential Trade Agreements (PTAs).
- **Requirement:** Correct Certificate of Origin (COO) documentation is essential to claim these benefits.

➢ **Customs Duty Drawback on Re-Exports**

- **Benefit:** If imported goods are re-exported within a specific period, customs duties paid on import can be refunded.
- **Common Issues:** Incorrect classification or missed deadlines can lead to claim rejection.

Why Businesses Miss Out on These Benefits?

➢ **Lack of Awareness & Rapid Policy Changes**: Government incentives are dynamic; staying updated requires continuous effort.

- **Errors in Documentation & Compliance**: Incorrect HS codes, missing declarations, or improper invoicing can cause claims to be denied.
- **Over-Reliance on CHAs & Freight Forwarders**: Many do not proactively apply for all eligible benefits.

How to Maximize Your Trade Incentives?

- **Monitor DGFT & CBIC Notifications**: Stay informed about updates to government policies, incentive structures, and procedural changes.
- **Cross-Verify CHA & Consultant Claims**: Ensure that all applications and documentation are filed accurately and in compliance with the latest regulations.
- **Work with Trade & Customs Experts**: Engaging professionals can help you **maximize duty savings, minimize compliance risks**, and uncover incentives you may have overlooked.

By actively tracking and optimizing trade incentives, businesses can significantly reduce costs, improve cash flow, and enhance profitability in global trade. Don't leave money on the table—start leveraging your trade benefits today!

CHAPTER 3

Proper Documentation Can Prevent Costly Customs Penalties in Imports & Exports

India's customs clearance process has become increasingly **digital, regulated, and unforgiving**, making accurate documentation absolutely essential for both importers and exporters. Even minor discrepancies in invoices, shipping bills, or bills of entry can lead to shipment delays, penalties, or loss of financial benefits such as duty exemptions, GST refunds, and export incentives.

Once customs documents are filed, corrections can be complex, time-consuming and costly, often requiring multiple approvals and increasing operational expenses. Errors such as mismatched HS codes, incorrect valuation, or missing compliance certificates can trigger customs audits, inspections, and even blacklisting in severe cases.

Case Studies: Costly Documentation Errors

- **Export Case: Navanya Textiles** (Real name withheld for confidentiality reasons)

  An Ahmedabad-based textile exporter faced a ₹50000 penalty and detention charges due to a mismatch between their invoice value and the declared FOB (Free on Board) value in the shipping bill. A simple manual data entry **mistake** led to a misdeclaration fine—one that could have easily been avoided through careful cross-verification.

- **Import Case: VoltX International** (Real name withheld for confidentiality reasons)

  A Mumbai-based electronics importer incurred a ₹3 lakh penalty when customs flagged an undervaluation error in their Bill of Entry. The mistake in CIF (Cost, Insurance, and Freight) value calculation resulted in a fine, highlighting the importance of accurate documentation.

Key Documentation Best Practices for Importers & Exporters

- **Work with Trained Staff or an Experienced Customs Broker**

  A knowledgeable and proactive customs agent can ensure all documentation is complete, accurate, and fully compliant with evolving regulations.

- **Use Automated Software for Document Management**

  Digital tools help reduce human errors, ensure consistency, and streamline the filing of crucial documents such as Bill of Lading, Commercial Invoices, Packing Lists, Shipping Bills, and Bills of Entry.

- **Verify HS Codes & Product Classification**

  Misclassification of goods can result in incorrect duties, customs rejections, or unnecessary inspections. Importers and exporters should regularly update HS codes as per DGFT and CBIC guidelines.

- **Ensure Compliance with Duty Exemptions & Export Promotion Schemes**

  Importers benefiting from schemes like EPCG (Export Promotion Capital Goods) and SEZ (Special Economic Zone) must maintain proper documentation to avoid penalties. Similarly, exporters under RoDTEP or Advance Authorisation must ensure correct paperwork to secure incentives.

- **Double-Check Bank & Financial Documentation**

  Errors in Letter of Credit (LC), bill of exchange, or foreign currency transactions can delay customs clearance and create compliance issues with RBI regulations.

- **Stay Updated on Changing Customs Policies**

  Regulations frequently evolve, impacting documentation requirements. Both importers and exporters should monitor CBIC and DGFT notifications to ensure compliance.

Final Thought

By following these documentation best practices, businesses can:

- Minimize financial and regulatory risks
- Ensure smooth and timely customs clearance
- Protect export incentives and tax benefits
- Build a trusted reputation in global trade

Don't let paperwork mistakes cost you your profits—treat documentation as a strategic priority.

CHAPTER 4

Mastering Incoterms: Prevent Hidden Costs & Trade Risks

Incoterms (International Commercial Terms) define the responsibilities of buyers and sellers in global trade, particularly in relation to **transportation, insurance, risk, and cost sharing**.

However, misunderstanding these terms can lead to unexpected costs, legal disputes, and shipment delays.

Indian exporters and importers, particularly SMEs, often accept Incoterms without fully analyzing their financial and logistical impact, leading to hidden expenses and operational disruptions.

Real-World Mistakes & Their Impact

- **IndoMach Exim Corporation** (fictitious name), a Mumbai-based machinery exporter, agreed to a **DAP (Delivered at Place)** contract without realizing they were responsible for all transportation costs up to the buyer's location, including local handling in a foreign country. When the buyer delayed customs clearance, the exporter had to pay **€1500 in detention** charges, reducing profitability.

- Similarly, GearGrid Exim LLP (fictitious name), an Indian auto parts importer agreed to CIF (Cost, Insurance & Freight) terms but failed to account for **local port handling and delivery charges** at the destination. The result? An unexpected **₹1.2 lakh** in documentation and unloading fees—expenses that could have been avoided with proper planning.

These examples underscore how Incoterms **directly impact your bottom line** and must be managed with attention and strategy.

Common Incoterms & Their Risks Exposure

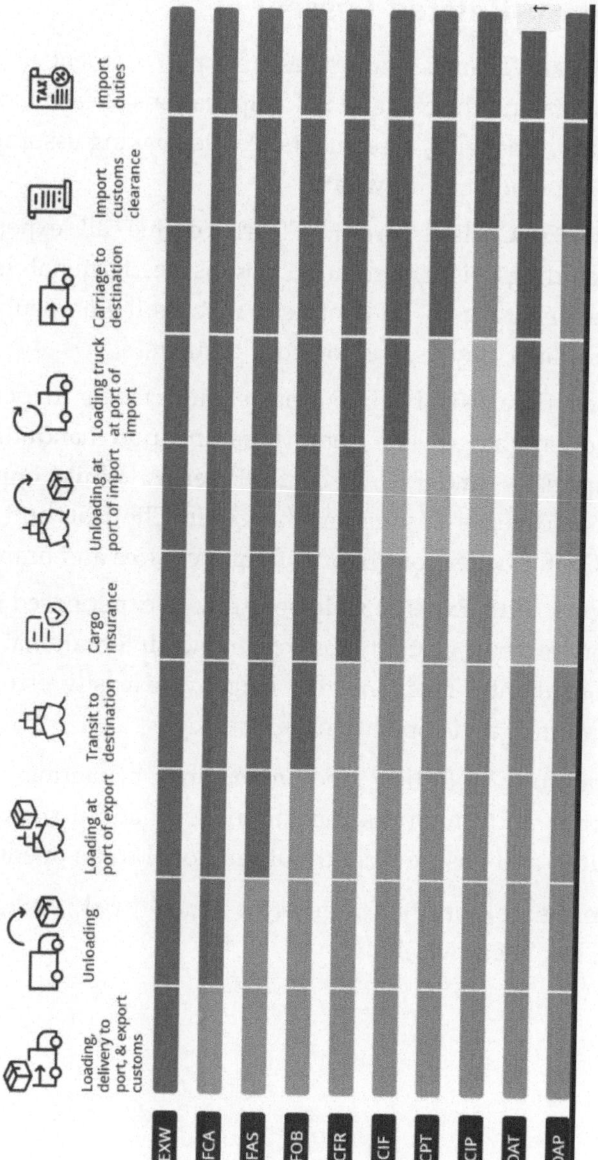

How Businesses Can Avoid Incoterm-Related Losses

- ☑ **Educate Teams:** Train sales and procurement teams to understand the cost and risk implications of each Incoterm before finalizing agreements. Avoid making assumptions about who pays for what.
- ☑ **Clarify Costs Upfront:** Clearly define all expenses—including freight, handling, customs fees, terminal charges, and insurance – in contracts. Discuss them openly with suppliers, buyers, and logistics partners.
- ☑ **Negotiate Wisely:** Exporters should factor in potential hidden charges like demurrage and port handling fees, especially under DAP or DDP terms. While importers should verify destination charges in CIF deals and prefer **FOB** for better control over freight choices and timing.
- ☑ **Work with Experts:** Collaborate with experienced freight forwarders, customs brokers, and international trade consultants. Their insights help avoid costly errors and optimize trade operational efficiency.

By carefully selecting and managing Incoterms, Indian exporters and importers can minimize financial risks, avoid disputes, and ensure smooth international trade operations.

Incoterms are more than trade terms—they're risk management tools. Use them wisely.

CHAPTER 5

How Unrealistic Commitments Drive Up Costs for Importers & Exporters

The Cost of Over-Commitment in Global Trade

In India's fast-paced trade environment, unrealistic commitments can lead to major financial losses. Businesses trying to impress buyers with tight delivery promises often overlook ground realities—leading to expensive last-minute actions.

- **SouthThread International** (Real name withheld for confidentiality reasons) a **Tirupur-based garment exporter** lost ₹3 lakh due to last-minute air-shipping caused by production delays.
- **Mumbex Global Solutions** (Real name withheld for confidentiality reasons) A **Mumbai-based importer** had to pay a heavy premium for urgent local sourcing after a delayed overseas shipment disrupted their supply chain.

These situations are not rare—they are recurring examples of **avoidable losses**. To stay profitable, businesses must **set**

realistic timelines, add buffers, communicate proactively, and diversify suppliers for smoother operations and sustained success.

The Hidden Cost Triggers

Last-Minute Air Freight Costs

- When shipments are delayed, businesses are often forced to switch to air freight, which is 5-7 times costlier than ocean freight.
- Emergency bookings come with premium surcharges, especially during peak seasons, further inflating costs.

Production & Supply Chain Disruptions

- Delays in imported raw materials or components slow down manufacturing, leading to increased labor costs, missed deadlines, and potential penalties.
- Rushing production due to tight schedules results in overtime wages, quality control failures, and even machine breakdowns.

Customs & Logistics Bottlenecks

- Indian supply chains depend on multiple stakeholders: **freight forwarders, customs agents, CFS operators, and transporters**.
- Even small errors or delays—like **port congestion, misfiled documents, or incomplete declarations**—can push shipments off schedule.
- Add to that **unexpected regulatory inspections** or **last-minute HS code clarifications**, and the entire delivery plan is jeopardized.

Loss of Buyer Trust & Market Share

- Repeated failure to meet promised timelines **damages credibility**.
- For exporters, this may lead to **canceled orders**, **delayed payments**, and **loss of repeat business**.
- For importers, **domestic customers or retailers** may impose penalties or shift to more reliable vendors.
- Some international contracts include strict SLAs (Service Level Agreements) - violations can be **costly both financially and reputationally**.

Winning Strategies: How Indian Businesses Can Avoid These Pitfalls

Set Realistic Timelines

- Factor in production lead times, supplier reliability, customs processes, and freight transit times before making delivery commitments.

Include Buffer Time

- Add a 10-15% margin to account for unexpected disruptions like transport strikes, supplier delays, or regulatory issues.

Communicate Proactively

- Keep buyers and suppliers informed about potential delays and offer alternative solutions, such as partial shipments, to minimize disruption.
- Proactive updates create **trust and transparency**, especially during delays.

Diversify Suppliers & Shipping Routes

- Avoid putting all your risk on a single source or logistics lane.
- Establish **backup vendors, alternate shipping routes**, or even **different ports of loading/unloading**.
- This flexibility helps you respond quickly when your primary route faces disruptions.

Final Insight

In international trade, **speed without strategy can be expensive**.

Unrealistic commitments may impress in the short term but damage margins, timelines, and trust in the long run.

Smart planning, communication, and contingency strategies help you **deliver on time, every time – without draining profits.**

Success in trade isn't about how fast you promise; it's about how smartly you prepare.

CHAPTER 6

Optimizing Shipment Modes for Indian Exporters & Importers

For Indian businesses engaged in global trade, selecting the right shipment mode is **not just a logistics decision – it's a cost and time management strategy**. The wrong choice can eat into margins, cause delays, and lead to poor customer experiences. Many exporters and importers still default to inland container depots (ICDs) without evaluating smarter alternatives like **factory stuffing, direct port delivery (DPD)**, or **bonded trucking.** This lack of evaluation often results in **avoidable expenses, extended lead times**, and reduced competitiveness.

By taking a strategic view of shipment planning, businesses can tailor their logistics to suit their cargo type, trade volume, and delivery timelines – achieving **maximum cost-efficiency, speed, and reliability.**

Case Study: Cost Savings Through Shipment Optimization

- **Pink Stone Global** (Real name withheld for confidentiality reasons) a Jaipur-based ceramic exporter initially routed all shipments through an ICD before transporting containers to Mundra Port. This added unnecessary handling and transit delays. By switching to factory stuffing and direct port delivery, they reduced shipping costs by 15% and minimized handling time.

- Similarly, **IndoSynth Exports & Imports** (Real name withheld for confidentiality reasons) a Delhi-based, chemical importer cleared all shipments through an ICD, incurring extra haulage and handling costs. After evaluating the flow, they shifted to **direct port delivery at Nhava Sheva and Mundra**. Last-mile transport was arranged from the port directly, resulting in **12% savings in logistics costs** and faster turnaround.

These case studies prove that a few smart decisions in shipment mode can unlock significant savings without compromising on delivery.

Key Factors to Consider When Selecting a Shipment Mode

1. **Total Cost Analysis**
    - Compare the overall cost, including freight rates, ICD handling fees, haulage charges, and port surcharges.
    - In some cases, direct port stuffing (for exports) and bonded trucking (for imports) help eliminate redundant ICD-related expense costs.
2. **Transit Time & Handling Risks**
    - Using ICDs can introduce additional handling steps, increasing the risk of cargo damage, delays, and detention charges.

- Direct port movement reduces multiple handling stages, leading to faster clearance and fewer risks.

3. **Port Proximity & Accessibility**
    - For factories located far from major ports, ICDs may still be the practical option.
    - However, exporters and importers in states like **Gujarat, Maharashtra, Tamil Nadu, and Andhra Pradesh** can benefit greatly from direct port access – saving on inland haulage and reducing turnaround times.

4. **Customs Clearance Efficiency**
    - Direct port deliveries often experience faster customs clearance, avoiding ICD-related delays.
    - However, **complex or high-risk shipments** (e.g., chemicals, electronics, or pharmaceuticals) may still require **ICD clearance** due to longer inspection protocols or facility availability.

Additional Tip: Shipment Mode Is Not One-Size-Fits-All

Different products, destinations, and seasons may require different approaches. For example:

- **Perishable goods** may need faster clearance and refrigerated handling – favoring port-side solutions.
- **Bulk cargo** may benefit from rail-linked ICDs that offer secure and efficient inland transport.

Proactively reviewing your shipment mode quarterly or during rate negotiations can unlock new savings and better service levels.

CHAPTER 7

Frequent Changes in Freight Forwarders & CHAs Can Disrupt Efficiency

In an attempt to cut costs, many Indian exporters and importers frequently switch freight forwarders or Customs House Agents (CHAs) to find the lowest rates. However, this strategy can backfire, leading to shipment delays, compliance issues, financial penalties, and damaged business relationships.

A **Hyderabad-based pharmaceutical exporter** suffered penalties when their newly appointed CHA misclassified goods under the wrong HS code, leading to customs delays and missed delivery deadlines. Similarly, a **Mumbai-based electronics importer** faced excessive duties and supply chain disruptions due to incorrect classification by a low-cost CHA unfamiliar with their product category.

Risks of Frequently Changing Freight Forwarders & CHAs

Delays Due to KYC & Compliance

- Every new CHAs must undergo **KYC verification**, which can cause delays in documentation and clearance.

- Inexperienced CHAs may lack knowledge of **sector-specific compliance**, such as requirements for pharmaceuticals, perishables, or high-value goods – leading to shipment hold-ups.

Documentation Errors & Customs Penalties

- Incorrect **HS code classification, missing documents, or misfiled duty benefits** can lead to financial penalties or shipment rejections.
- Capital Looms International (fictitious name), a **Delhi-based textile importer**, was fined due to misdeclared tariff benefits, while Madras MotorParts Exports (fictitious name), a **Chennai-based auto parts exporter**, lost their RODTEP refund due to documentation lapses.

Lack of Understanding of Product & Market Requirements

- Long-term CHAs understand **duty exemptions, compliance requirements, and optimal shipping strategies** for specific industries.
- Freshroots Global Pvt. Ltd. (fictitious name), a **Chennai-based food importer**, lost an entire consignment of perishable goods due to incorrect **FSSAI clearance**, while Nextronix Exports LLP, an **electronics exporter in Bengaluru**, faced delays when their new forwarder booked an inefficient carrier.

Inconsistent Freight Rates & Service Quality

- New freight forwarders may offer **low initial rates but impose hidden charges** (handling, warehousing, etc.).

- PitStop Exim Pvt. Ltd. (fictitious name), a **Pune-based auto parts importer**, incurred **demurrage charges** due to delayed customs clearance by an inexperienced CHA.

Best Practices for Importers & Exporters

- **Build Long-Term Relationships**: Reliable CHAs ensure smoother operations, fewer compliance issues, and better service quality.
- **Choose Experienced Partners**: Work with logistics providers specializing in your product category.
- **Negotiate Competitive Rates**: Instead of switching frequently, **negotiate long-term contracts** with performance-based pricing and service-level agreements.
- **Audit CHA Compliance Regularly**: Conduct periodic checks on documentation, duty claims, and HS classifications.

By focusing on **stability, compliance, and strategic** partnerships rather than short-term cost-cutting, businesses can minimize risks, ensure seamless customs clearance, and optimize their global trade operations.

CHAPTER 8

Smart Shipment Tracking: A Must for Indian Exporters & Importers

In today's fast-paced global trade environment, shipment tracking is no longer optional—it's essential. Yet many Indian exporters and importers, especially SMEs, still rely on manual updates from freight forwarders, customs agents, or suppliers. This lack of real-time visibility leads to delays, miscommunication, and financial losses due to penalties or supply chain disruptions.

The Problem: Unreliable Manual Tracking

- **For Exporters:** KnitCore International (fictitious name), a Ludhiana-based garment exporter lost buyer trust when delayed shipment updates caused a missed delivery deadline. Manual tracking led to miscommunication, strained relationships, and potential future business loss.
- **For Importers:** Nexonic Import Solution (fictitious name), a Mumbai-based electronics importer faced production halts due to delayed shipment updates from a Chinese supplier. With no real-time tracking in place, the team faced stockouts, idle labor, and financial setbacks.

Without digital tracking, businesses face:

✕ **Uncertainty in Estimated Arrival Times (ETA)**: Buyers and production teams are left in the dark and forced to follow up repeatedly.

✕ **Risk of Penalties & Extra Costs**: Demurrage, detention, customs delays, and warehousing charges increase when shipments go unmonitored.

✕ **Operational Disruptions**: Unexpected transit delays impact inventory, production, and customer commitments.

The Solution: Invest in Digital Shipment Tracking

Real-time shipment tracking enables businesses to:

- ➢ Monitor cargo at every stage
- ➢ Identify bottlenecks early
- ➢ Communicate proactively with all stakeholders
- ➢ Make timely operational decisions

How Exporters & Importers Can Implement Smart Tracking

☑ **Use Digital Tracking Platforms**

- Major shipping lines and freight forwarders offer tracking tools.
- Platforms like **(Shiprocket, Freightify, CargoX, SHIP GO)** and others provide real-time container and cargo visibility.
- Some ERP and TMS systems now integrate tracking directly into business dashboards.

☑ **Enhance Transparency with Buyers & Suppliers**

- **Exporters:** Share tracking links or system-generated updates with buyers to build confidence and reduce unnecessary follow-ups.
- **Importers:** Ask suppliers to provide tracking IDs as soon as goods are dispatched.

☑ **Leverage GPS & IoT for High-Value or Sensitive Goods**

- IoT-enabled trackers are ideal for temperature-controlled goods like **pharmaceuticals, perishables, and electronics**.
- GPS-based container tracking ensures better route visibility, especially for high-value cargo or multimodal shipments.

☑ **Work with Tech-Enabled Logistics Partners**

- Choose freight forwarders or CHA firms that offer **digital dashboards, milestone alerts**, and integration with systems like **ICEGATE** (Indian Customs) and **PCS** (Port Community Systems).
- Opt for partners who offer **predictive analytics** based on transit trends, ETAs, and port congestion alerts.

Key Benefits of Smart Shipment Tracking

➢ **Faster & Transparent Communication**: Reduces the need to chase forwarders and suppliers.

➢ **Lower Risk of Delays & Extra Costs**: Proactive tracking helps avoid penalties and disruptions.

➢ **Improved Supplier & Buyer Confidence**: Strengthens relationships and secures repeat business.

- **Optimized Inventory & Production**: Businesses can plan better and prevent stock shortages or excess.

In global trade, visibility equals control.

Smart shipment tracking not only prevents loss – it builds trust, efficiency, and competitive advantage in every transaction.

CHAPTER 9

Empowering Indian Trade: The Importance of Logistics Training

In global trade, Indian businesses focus on competitive pricing, shipping efficiency, and regulatory compliance. However, one crucial area is frequently overlooked: **training logistics staff.**

Without proper training, even the best strategies can fall apart—leading to:

- Shipment delays
- Compliance violations
- Hidden costs
- Damaged client relationships

In logistics, even a small mistake can have a **large ripple effect** across the supply chain.

Why Logistics Training Matters

A well-trained team ensures **accurate documentation, cost-effective shipping, and regulatory compliance.**

On the other hand, lack of training exposes businesses to **avoidable penalties, inefficiencies, and reputational loss.**

- **Export Example:** Sutradhar Global Textiles, a Delhi-based textile exporter faced regular customs delays due to incorrect HS codes entries. After investing in employee training, clearance time improved significantly—resulting in **cost savings and smoother buyer experiences.**
- **Import Example:** Mumbai Bijli Bazaar, a Mumbai-based electronics importer incurred high duties due to misclassification. With targeted training, their team corrected the valuation process, **cutting import expenses and avoiding repeated issues.**

Common Challenges Faced by Untrained Staff

- ⦸ **Incorrect Documentation**: Leads to penalties and shipment holds.
- ⦸ **Misunderstanding Incoterms**: Results in unplanned freight costs, disputes, and margin loss.
- ⦸ **Inefficient Freight Planning**: Poor coordination increases shipping time, costs, and handling errors.
- ⦸ **Lack of Trade Regulation Awareness**: Missed opportunities in duty exemptions, and risks of non-compliance with DGFT or Customs rules.

How Businesses Can Strengthen Training

☑ **Invest in Training Programs**

Conduct in-house sessions and collaborate with industry bodies like:

- **FIEO (Federation of Indian Export Organisations)**
- **EXIM Bank**
- **CII (Confederation of Indian Industry)**

☑ **Use Online Resources & Trade Workshops**

Platforms like **Niryat Bandhu** offer free training on trade documentation and compliance.

Also attend **DGFT and Customs webinars, trade expos, and compliance summits.**

☑ **Stay Updated on Regulations**

Regularly follow updates from:

- **DGFT (Directorate General of Foreign Trade)**
- **ICEGATE (Indian Customs EDI Gateway)**
- **CBIC (Central Board of Indirect Taxes and Customs)**

☑ **Create Internal SOPs & Learning Modules**

Make training ongoing, not one-time. Build Standard Operating Procedures (SOPs), quick-reference guides, and review modules to ensure learning stays fresh.

Key Benefits of Training

- ➢ **Fewer shipment delays & penalties**
- ➢ **Lower logistics costs through better decisions**
- ➢ Improved compliance and faster clearances
- ➢ **Stronger trade relationships & smoother operations**
- ➢ **A more confident and efficient operations team**

Logistics training isn't an expense—it's a **strategic investment** for growth in global trade. Whether exporting or importing, a **skilled team** ensures seamless operations and competitive success.

CHAPTER 10

Beyond Price: Choosing the Right Freight Forwarder for Smooth Exports & Imports

Many Indian businesses, particularly small and medium enterprises, often prioritize the lowest freight rates when selecting a logistics partner. While this may seem cost-effective initially, choosing a freight forwarder based **solely on price** can lead to **shipment delays, compliance issues, hidden charges**, and **poor service quality**—often costing much more in the long run.

In global trade, a cheap freight rate without accountability can become the most expensive mistake.

Whether you are an **importer or exporter**, selecting the **right freight forwarder** is essential for ensuring smooth, compliant, and reliable international operations.

The Hidden Costs of Cheap Freight Services:

🚨 **Case Study: Export Failure Due to Low-Cost Forwarder**
Deshbandhu Exports LLP, a Baroda-based exporter, chose the cheapest freight forwarder without verifying their credibility. The forwarder outsourced the shipment to a

middleman, leading to misrouting and customs clearance issues.

Result: ₹3 lakhs in penalties and storage charges – completely wiping out any profit in shipment.

🚨 **Common Issues with Low-Cost Freight Forwarders**

- ✕ **Hidden Charges**: Low upfront rates often mask additional fees for customs clearance, warehousing, handling, port charges, and document preparation.
- ✕ **Unreliable Service**: Many low-cost forwarders offer limited tracking, poor customer service, and inconsistent delivery timelines—affecting your business commitments.
- ✕ **Poor Documentation Handling**: Incorrect paperwork can lead to customs holds, fines, or even cargo seizure.
- ✕ **Middlemen & Subcontracting**: Some freight forwarders pass shipments through multiple hands, increasing the risk of mismanagement and lack of accountability.

How to Choose the Right Freight Forwarder

☑ **Prioritize Reliability & Experience Over Cost**

- Look for forwarders with proven expertise in your domain—**textiles, pharmaceuticals, auto components, electronics, or chemicals.**
- Ensure they offer specialized handling (DG cargo, temperature-sensitive, etc.) and manage both **air and sea freight** efficiently.

☑ **Verify Transparency & Accountability**

- Always request a **detailed quote** outlining each component of the cost.
- Confirm if the forwarder **manages shipments directly** or outsources to third parties.
- Ask about their liability policies in case of damage or loss.

☑ **Request References & Case Studies**

- A professional forwarder should readily provide **case studies** or client references from similar industries.
- Speaking to their existing clients gives real-world insight into service consistency and professionalism.

☑ **Check for Digital Tracking & Communication**

- Real-time tracking platforms and **automated shipment updates** reduce follow-ups and ensure peace of mind.
- Choose a partner with **responsive communication,** escalation support, and a dedicated point of contact.

Final Thought

Freight forwarding is not just a **service**—it's a **strategic partnership** that affects your **costs, timelines, compliance, and customer satisfaction**.

Choose wisely. A trustworthy freight forwarder will not only ship your goods but also protect your profits, reputation, and peace of mind.

Smart Logistics: The Game-Changer for Indian Exporters & Importers

In today's fast-paced global trade environment, **logistics is more than just transportation**—it's a strategic tool that fuels **profitability, efficiency, and business growth**. Whether you're an **Indian exporter** aiming for **faster deliveries and competitive pricing** or an **importer** ensuring **a smooth supply chain**, smart logistics is the secret weapon to **stay ahead in the market**.

✷ Why Smart Logistics is a Must-Have:

☑ **Cut Costs, Boost Profits**: Poor logistics planning leads to **higher freight costs, demurrage, detention, and customs penalties**. Smart supply chain strategies help eliminate wasteful expenses and optimize every rupee spent.

☑ **Never Miss a Deadline**: Delays don't just cost money-they damage relationships and brand reputation. Efficient logistics ensures timely movement, even in unpredictable market conditions.

☑ **Stay 100% Compliant**: Small documentation mistakes can snowball into customs delays, fines, or even shipment seizure. Proactive logistics keeps your business on the right side of the law.

☑ **Build Stronger Business Relationships**: Reliable deliveries build buyer trust, while efficient imports help maintain supplier confidence and consistency—two pillars of long-term trade success.

🚢 Key Strategies for Smarter Logistics

💡 Plan Your Shipments Like a Pro

- Compare shipping modes (Air vs. Sea, LCL vs. FCL) based on **urgency, volume, and cost**.
- Consolidate shipments to **cut per-unit logistics expenses.**
- Avoid last-minute airfreight **rush fees** that eat into profits.

💡 Choose Partners That Deliver More Than Just Shipments

- Don't just go for the **cheapest freight forwarder—experience & reliability matter.**
- ✓ Build **long-term partnerships** for **consistent service & reduced delays.**

💡 Unlock Government Incentives & Save Big

- **Exporters**: Benefit from **Duty Drawback, RODTEP, and EPCG** to reduce costs.
- ✓ **Importers**: Leverage **EPCG, IGCR, and concessional duty schemes.**

💡 **Power Up with Tech & Real-Time Tracking**

- **Use smart tracking tools** for live shipment visibility & fewer surprises.
- **Automate paperwork & compliance** to cut human errors & delays.

Import Strategy, Export Smiles

Thank you for giving your valuable time and finishing this book.

You've just explored what's almost like a **Wikipedia of smart logistics for Indian exporters and importers**—with real stories, common mistakes, and practical solutions.

Now, you have two choices:

1. You can take this book as your map and walk the path alone.

Or

2. If you'd prefer to have me by your side—whether to clarify something, guide you through a challenge, or simply share thoughts—you're welcome to schedule a **1-to-1 meeting** with me.

Drop me a message at **Deepak@fluidglobal.co.in** and we'll take it forward from there.

Let's simplify logistics together—step by step.

Your Friendly Logistics Expert,

Deepak Bhadwarya